High Heels & Sneakers:
My Balance Myth

poems by

Nancy Kerrigan

Finishing Line Press
Georgetown, Kentucky

High Heels & Sneakers: My Balance Myth

*For Our Daughter, Ellen,
in this way you may stay "forever young."*

Copyright © 2017 by Nancy Kerrigan
ISBN 978-1-63534-120-1 First Edition
All rights reserved under International and Pan-American Copyright Conventions.
No part of this book may be reproduced in any manner whatsoever without written permission from the publisher, except in the case of brief quotations embodied in critical articles and reviews.

ACKNOWLEDGMENTS

I wish to express my appreciation to those Editors who have published my poems.

"Hand-Me-Downs" & "The Mack House" *A Place For What Was*. Grayson Books, 2014
"Behind Closed Doors" *Caduceus*, Vol. 8, 2010.
"What Saves Us" *The Voices: The Poetry of Psychiatry*. Finishing Line Press. 2009.
"Empty Boots." & "For the Women Who Ride Buses" *Kalliope*. Vol. XXIX, 2007.
"The Purple Metallic Convertible." *From The Frost Place: The Breath of Parted Lips*. Vol. II. 2004.
"The Writer & The Warriors" *Long River Run*. 2009.

Publisher: Leah Maines

Editor: Christen Kincaid

Cover Art: public domain

Author Photo: Bill Crofton at Moto Photo, Avon, CT

Cover Design: Elizabeth Maines

Printed in the USA on acid-free paper.
Order online: www.finishinglinepress.com
also available on amazon.com

Author inquiries and mail orders:
Finishing Line Press
P. O. Box 1626
Georgetown, Kentucky 40324
U. S. A.

Table of Contents

Off Script
Hope Is 1
The Purple Metallic Convertible 2
Off Script 4
Eastern Adulterer 5

Sneakers
Dancing or Jogging in Place 6
Mama Drama 7
One Dog Woman 9
Second Stories 10
Behind Closed Doors 12
Photographs 13
Hand-Me-Downs 14

High Heels
The Door 15
What Saves Us 17
The Rocker 18
Rough Days 19
New Season 20

Empty Boots
For the Women Who Ride Buses 21
Men Working 22
Empty Boots 24
The Writer & the Warriors 25
We're Still Here 27

Flip Flops
How to Have a Memorable Summer Vacation 28
Wimbledon, England 29
We Turn Sixty on Nantucket 30
Viewing the Pieta 31

September's Prayer
The Mack House 32
Mother of the Bride Ejected From Convertible 33
Sonnet During a Storm 34
Dinner with Friends 35
September's Prayer 36

OFF SCRIPT

HOPE IS

leaving all you love and hate
driving from the Midwest
in a Japanese compact car
a sewing machine
for an engine
buttons for wheels
at midlife with all needed
possessions behind you
family photos, a tennis racket
favorite albums and tapes
across that run-on-sentence
of a state, Pennsylvania
for a job the natives won't take;

witnessing a double rainbow
colors exquisite in the gray
mountain fog, beeping
at unknown drivers to look
beyond their low beams

believing a new life awaits.

OFF SCRIPT

THE PURPLE METALLIC CONVERTIBLE

was the last loaner on the lot
on a top down day in May.
With the family sedan safely
in the mechanic's hands, I peeled
away from the dealership.
Convertibles automatically subtract
ten years off your driver's license.
Midlife mother became *Lolita* in sunglasses
with blond hair flying in a car I'd never pick.
Driver's honked as my briefcase
Bounced to the *Beach Boys:*
… *fun, fun, fun 'til her Daddy*
takes her T-Bird away…
sometimes a day just takes you.

Sometimes a day just takes you, like
a one hundred dollar bill in the envelope day
or a sudden call from a long lost lover day
that takes you to a secret room in yourself
and you burst right through its closed door

in a purple metallic convertible
with the *Beach Boys* blarin'
and you do something you have never
done before, like blow off a work day,
or spend all the money on yourself,
or go out with the married man.

And even if it rained all day on the beach,
or the money only purchased unlucky lottery tickets,
or the long lost lover was nothing more than an oil slick
that night in the convertible
with your hair hung over the head rest
while you are gazing at the moonlit night

OFF SCRIPT

you feel satisfied that you sampled
the cookies when they were passed
that you searched around that room
you never explored.

Sometimes we just need to shift into another gear.

OFF SCRIPT

OFF SCRIPT

Actors
brilliant and not
know off script.
Lines forgotten
an exit or entrance
missed.
No one picks up
your cue.
You blush.
There's a hush.
You want to be
behind the curtain
off stage.

Can't give
my life today
a rave review.
Not the comedy
I wished, but
not a cliché.
Not my first draft.
I improvise
project lies.
Where's my lead
my co-star?
What are my lines?
What do I wear
with every morning
opening night?
Where do I go
in this one woman show?

OFF SCRIPT

EASTERN ADULTERER

It's been years since we've lived together, Chicago.
You, the Second City, my first love. My regular guy.
Neck of your rented tuxedo shirt unbuttoned, tie loosened.
In gilded ballrooms, like old movie sets, we danced 'til dawn
sped down Lake Shore Drive, parked to see the sun rise.

You, the city of good men. The Sandburgs, Carl and Ryne.
The Richard Daleys, all living side by side. Home of the Cubs
the Sox, the Bulls, and the Bears, where winners & losers
are loved just the same. City of riots, schemes and scandals
where passersby will look you straight in the eye.

Your skyline never recedes, becomes more beautiful with age.
Skyscrapers that loom out of the lake, my big brothers
ready to protect me. City of big shoulders, near which I laid
my head each night, I left your weathered, unshaven face
fearful the passion had drained from our forty year marriage.

Soon Hartford's Brooks Brothers bureaucrats were breathing down
my neck. Suitable men turned into aetnoids by the world of insurance.
Actuarial tables more important than musical scales.
Any city with two writer's houses in a row
a luxury for literary high brows. In the *Sunken Garden*
poets wooed me with words that gently kissed my cheeks.

Captivated by quaint New England charm, awed by brainy schools
and good looks, I've become an eastern adulterer, sleeping
here for awhile, savoring each fall, never awakening
in a bed that feels like my own, arising each morning
thinking maybe it's time to move on. Or is it time to go home?

SNEAKERS

DANCING OR JOGGING IN PLACE

In Mother's era of silk stockings
the elegance of the dark seams drew
the onlooker's eyes up and down
as if reading unpunctuated sentences.
Even as they dried in the bathroom
they looked graceful, like resting
Rockettes. She pulled them on one leg
at a time, foot arched, toes pointed
ballerina style. She stepped into her days
danced into her evenings
in three inch high heels.

My morning kicks off with the ritual
of stuffing myself into a pair of pantyhose.
It's like trying to put
toothpaste back into the tube.
Once they're on, some pairs are so long
they ripple and fold in the fashion of elephant flesh.
Others so short, I feel like a contestant in a sack race.

My ten hour day ends when I rip them off.
Oohs and ahs follow, as I jam both legs
into my sweats at the same time
tie up my ragged sneakers.
As these articles of female constriction
lie in a puddle on the bedroom floor
my legs warm with the return of blood flow.
You'll hear cries
G-L-O-R-I-A, G-L-O-R-I-A
Gloria!

SNEAKERS

MAMA DRAMA

Act I.

Criminal torture, my daughter griped about the sound
coming from her bathroom toilet. I bent the arm
of the floating ball in the tank, as directed in my
New York Times Guide To Home Repair, a divorce gift.
A geyser zoomed upward, the tank lid rose three feet.
Water squirted into her bedroom and soaked my sweats.
My sneakers squeaked as I went to greet Joe, the plumber & his son.
It was a holiday. Appliances keep track of holidays.
As Joe & I searched the house for the shut off valve
his son negotiated a prom date with my daughter.
Do it again, Mom!

Act II.

This time flooring issues drove me to my knees.
By now my high school senior & I were working together
like two students climbing the same staircase.
Large strips of carpet, shoved with our shoulders
in the direction of her bedroom door. We lodged a six foot
ball of the wall to wall wool in her doorway, not an easy task.
Neither of us were ever exiting the room until I light-bulbed
the idea of gently lowering her out her bedroom window.
Don't call the authorities yet, it was a ranch house.
Go get Painless, our next door dentist.
He's good at extractions.
Mom, someday I'll walk a Red carpet.

SNEAKERS

Act III

It was a smooth transition from *Playdoh* to cookie dough.
Baking together became our Christmas tradition. Never again
would I substitute *crème d' menthe* in the recipe for rum ball cookies.
That year no one binged on them due to their green tinge.
They remained in the cookie tin until March.
These escapades come back to me the way my inside out umbrella did
that Christmas, when I let the wind take it where it would.
A Good Samaritan returned it. It all comes back to me, her dreams
these one act days, where for a brief moment in time she was all mine.
My daughter and I unbroken in our broken world.

SNEAKERS

ONE DOG WOMAN

As children my mother diagnosed us with pet allergies.
I never wanted a goldfish, let alone a 6 month old
white wire-haired fox terrier. House broken on her resume.
No other canine crossed my threshold after I smuggled
Muffy, my first puppy into our home in the dark of night.
Our gift on our daughter's sixth birthday. I am a one dog woman.

A five foot cyclone fence, no deterrent for her—vaulted
from a squatting start. Her afternoon jaunts to the park
stimulated by a mere sniff of spring. Routine searches
ended when panting owner found panting pooch under
the shade of an oak tree. Summoned from work
I would collapse with her on scented grass.

We bred her with Snuggles, a local cad who did little else.
Never once sent child support for their four puppies.
The mysteries of birthing, the pain of having offspring
should not be denied any species—we reasoned. Me,
the proud midwife as the neighbor children observed
delivery sitting atop the washer & dryer in the kitchen.

Not one to discriminate, Muffy greeted all with licks
with leaps to both cheeks. I imagine the burglar
struggled as he departed with my precious jewelry
in his bag for Muffy hated when company left in a rush.
She lived a long life even by doggie standards.

Daughter away at college, we wrote her obit by phone:
Beloved wife of Snuggles, survived by Spunky, Ringo.
On a walk back to my noiseless home, still thinking
of my gadabout, I ask myself, is the sequel ever better
than the original? Do we ever forget our first love?

SNEAKERS

SECOND STORIES
Beverly Hills, Chicago

Mid-century builders raised me, a ranch, brick by brick on Longwood Drive.
For years I gazed up at Pill Hill, at it's oversized Georgians and Tudors owned by doctors who fled them in white flight. Chicago's last castle* only two blocks away.
My curmudgeons, whose cat ate only caviar, sold me for less than I was worth. That hurt.

Innocent of my leaking roof, the Green family mortgaged me, in love with my corner picture windows. My view spanned both directions of the Drive lined with elms & pines. In winter they wore petticoats. The Drive, a speed trap for drag racing high school kids, provided me and them with a bit of nightly excitement.

My family's terrier and I got bored one summer day. We let in burglars. Their pillowcases suggested a scavenger hunt. What a ruckus. Drawers yanked out of their chests.
Near-sighted robbers overlooked my secret closet in a closet, the sterling but not the Missus' diamond. Windows locked tightly, I couldn't breathe. It was house arrest for me.

E.J., their only child, skated my long driveway, celebrated birthdays, had friends in day & night, once without her parents home.
Dancing feet tickled my hardwood.
Born To Run played as Mom lost her balance on a sea of shoes in my foyer shooing the teens to the street. Later the teens were invited back for a chaperoned punishment party.

SNEAKERS

Those, my glory days. My fireplace forever burning, helped me survive endless Chicago winters. The '78 one so dreadful
they had my roof shoveled. Thank heavens, I thought I'd collapse.
My walls held them together. When E.J. left for college, her parents went their separate ways.
Couldn't say why, never heard any arguments.

Why do my families leave me? Am I showing my age? Because my plumbing won't work like a young home? My newest owners removed the roof to build on a huge second story. The blue sky my ceiling for awhile,
the kitchen became a tea cup. It made the old Mrs. cry when she visited.
She whispered in my mailbox as she left, I loved you the best.

* *Built by the architect Givens in 1886, modeled after a castle in Ireland*

SNEAKERS

BEHIND CLOSED DOORS

How pleasant not to be married this Valentine's Day, not
to wonder whether some guy will buy my favorite flowers.
What a relief not to arise to the salute of the toilet seat.
How grand not to stumble over a chocolate brown leather
Lazy Boy recliner on my way to bring in the newspaper.
From now on I'm the sole owner of the remote.

There is however the not so small matter of the queen- size bed,
the size and temperature of the Alaskan tundra. In dreams
I cavort with the likes of Robert Redford, into whose arms
I float 'til morning, which stomps in like a collection agent
demanding overdue mortgage payments, that are all mine.

Then again, the closets are my own. They come with doors
for a reason. All manner of secrets are hiding in them. Gowns
I dream I will fit into, boxes of love letters I can't let go.
I gaze at the wedding dress that outlived the groom, wondering
if it dances with his ghost to the long playing records
after the doors are closed and the lights are out.

It is four a.m. the darkest part of the night, when any sound
kicks one's imagination into overdrive. I hear a crash coming from
the closet, one, maybe two, glasses smashed against the wall. Next,
the rustle of fabric, the sound of soft shoes shuffling on hardwood
floors to the slow, plaintiff notes of Johnny Mathis singing...
Stay funny valentine stay...each day is Valentine's Day...

PHOTOGRAPHS

A photograph taken
upon my return
from a long unwanted separation
shows my arm encircling you.
At least, if absence
happened again
you'd remember me.
You stand in my lap
grasping a strand of my long hair
between your tiny fingers.
Your blond head touches mine.
You, my love,
in a navy sailor dress, no smile
torn between hello and goodbye.

Now, your photographic
image hides in a darkroom
sunken in a tray
of developing fluid.
Hazel eyes stare at its ceiling.
Something's amiss
the process goes backward.
Your bright smile floats away.
Eyes fade, disappear off a white page.
Thick chestnut hair strings off
into shoelaces. Arms folded
across your chest
almost erased
resolved not to embrace.

We are held together by a too thin thread.

SNEAKERS

HAND-ME-DOWNS

Layers of disappointment
keep the mothers warm.
A winter storm after years
of temperate weather.

My daughter throws a snow ball
as we adore my granddaughters
gliding and shuffling around the rink
shiny new ice skates gleaming.
Your hand-me-downs,
that's all I had.

Sadness follows me
all the way home.
Icicles hang from the gutter
tears dangling in midstream
frozen in time.
The house cries
to come in from the cold.
I'm ready to run out
to the sporting goods store, barefoot
plaid flannel nightgown and all
to buy new white figure skates
for a forty-year-old mother of two.

The account book of her childhood,
not fully funded. The payload
of parental guilt never overdrawn.

The old skates weren't so bad, Mom.
My friends saw Nancy Kerrigan's
autograph inside them.

HIGH HEELS

THE DOOR

opens slightly, as you learn
what brings them here, their journey.
Make friends with quiet, your own
theirs and the politeness of beginnings.

Crossing & uncrossing your legs to get
comfortable, to change your perspective
then invite them to change theirs.

In time, the story, the gush of pain
each word, paddles that start, have
scarred or hardened the heart.

Rub your eyes, sift through your own
unspoken memoir, check yourself
while the sand drifts down the hour glass.

Be the scrim for this drama, see many sides
yet filter the sadness, part the fog, direct
the water deepening in such a small space.

Listen, connect notes, what you hear, don't,
what's off key. What refrain keeps coming
back, or do they need to change their tune?

Life, a woven cloth, pull a thread, change
the pattern. When some threads unravel, you
stitch, you patch, reattach the severed parts.

HIGH HEELS

The door clicks shut. You collapse in
your chair. Breathe, take a deep breath
wrap both your arms around yourself

open your window to the real world.
See the sun, watch the snow, smell the rain
look over roof tops.

Next patient...

HIGH HEELS

WHAT SAVES US

*Come home now, Mom, Betty's swallowed
all of her Mother's heart medicine!*

The cicadas were ticking, marking time.
Daylight dimming as I barreled up the driveway.
I was the never home neighbor nurse
who never knew that next door Betty
could not see it through
could not take it
could not ignore
her life of sacrifice any more.

Cops and our teenage daughters
huddled between the homes.
White and wobbling like a bowling pin
Betty held off the men in blue serge
with a can of mace cocked
behind the side door's screen.
I slipped in the front door
held Betty; the cop grabbed the mace.
Her pulse, a weak drum beat
on our march out to the squad car.

Captor and captive were caged
in the back seat of a stalled cruiser that
could not get away
could not get out of its own way
could not get down the driveway
could not get down the street.
The heavy hot August night and
the noxious engine fumes choked her.
Our laps were soon warmed
by a blanket of Betty's vomit.

Streetlights, moonlight, city blue search light
home again from the hospital.
A nightingale sang.

HIGH HEELS

THE ROCKER

Tonight, exiting my office
I notice my chair is still rocking.
Does your ghost occupy it after I leave?
My chair in which no one else sits.
My chair which comforts me
as I spend my day listening to others.
A patient asked, *Do you sing lullabies too?*

An unfinished rocker we bought together long ago.
Stain you brushed on then, now worn off its edges.
This, our first purchase meant for a mother & child
who had not met yet. You became a father in it too.
It waltzed from the family room to my office
when I had a home office. Later it rocked
in rented offices in another state
as I practiced my profession

Now, I imagine you are here with me each day.
Its arms your arms, holding me
as I faced limits, my own & others.
Will it keep rocking until I retire?
I'd like to shrink it down to doll house size.
Have a friend place it on my grave, so the strong
breezes of the *Windy City* will keep it rocking,
since I won't be buried next to you.

HIGH HEELS

ROUGH DAYS, 2009
Inspired by Rough Day, 2005 by Jim Rennert

The resting figure, a bronze sculpture on a gallery pedestal
a Lincolnesque form in a great chair. It's a businessman
neck tie loosened, right arm resting on the arm of a stuffed chair.
Right hand a fist, slightly closed as if ready to fight. Left arm
of this man slung over the chair, knuckles nearly touching a floor.
His head stretched way back. Adam's apple pointing towards
the ceiling of an imagined home, his only haven.

Imagine another sculpture, the chair occupied by a woman in a suit
slouching on a kitchen chair. High heels totally kicked off.
One shoe toppled over on its side. A brief case opened in front of her
documents tumbling out, as if she'd try to catch up at home.
Her suit jacket & shoulder bag would hang from both edges of this chair.
At her side, a boy and a girl, stand with their mouths open
in hunger or complaint, or to demand a hug.

These sculptures could be right next to each other.
Fully equal, forged by ideals, necessity, weary from uncivil wars
with bodies that look as if they have run races organized by others.
But they cannot speak to one another of longings, of jobs or the loss of
them, cannot make hands meet, or ends meet.
Arms too stiff to hold the kids.
Nor can they gaze at the waxing moon, or out the windows
of their mortgaged home. The world they dwell in is running on empty.

HIGH HEELS

NEW SEASON

A mahogany clock on my office window sill stopped
whether a.m. or p.m., a mystery. It commanded my every moment.

The chill of a new season crept through the slightly open windows.
The book shelves stood as vacant as a toothless smile.

The gutted beige metal file cabinets rattled when shut, sounding
like empty wagons. Did they foreshadowed an empty mind?

My password no longer activated the grimy computer.
Black phone blessedly dead silent.

Standing there in sneakers and nylons, in the slim skirt
of my work suit, I slid my name out of the door plate,

trying to remove some core of myself. I grabbed a hooded
sweatshirt left by a patient to protect against the coming cold.

Time was still ticking, but in a secret chamber of my heart.
I did not know whether to mourn, file a grievance, or book a cruise.

EMPTY BOOTS

FOR THE WOMEN WHO RIDE BUSES

Rosa, since 1955 you've sat, and sat, and sat
in our minds on that Montgomery city bus

would not give up your seat to a white man.
You weren't the first black woman who refused

to go to the back of the bus, but you are the one
etched in the black and white of our memory.

You sat there dignified in your cloth coat
with your hat on, staring out of that bus window.

Were you planning dinner under that hat,
plotting to change history, or just plain tired?

How many bus rides did it take to make you seethe
steam rising up through your straw pill box

before you decided not to move? Your own name
not among the P's in my 1980 encyclopedia.

In that decade of *Father Knows Best*, my mother worked
outside the home too, wearing a hat much like yours.

Often she neglected to take it off while she cooked dinner.
Mornings, she ran in high heels to catch her two buses

consumed one library book after the next, the commute so long.
Some days rain washed away her makeup, or was it rain?

Thanks to the women who traveled unfamiliar routes before me
I drive to my own office where I listen to the plight of women

not behind the wheels of their lives, waiting in the rain
for buses to take them to the night shift at Walmart.

EMPTY BOOTS

MEN WORKING

Hard hats stand among orange cones.
One with a hand on a stick, *slow down* written on it.
The other hand pats down the summer air. Semis swoosh by.
He leans into the downdraft, turning like a weather vane.

Linemen perched on my telephone poles, legs stretched out
like Baryshnikov. Their bare hands connect wired circuitry
complex as our nervous system. I peek from behind the front blinds.
Bet they could ignite a spark or two in me.

Those city guys that cross high rise girders, how do they catch
their breath to whistle? Of course it's only for me. Arms open wide
as they go heel to toe across the tightrope of beams, hands steady.
Onlookers face upward, all eyes fixed, our lips moving in prayer.

The rescuers who come upon us to save us from ourselves.
The cop's hand crosses my open car window, brushing my cheek.
Our eyes lock and stare. His hand grabs mine as I turn over my license.
Ma'am, do you know how fast you're going? I hear how fast we're going.

Knee surgeons, the carpenters of medicine, mine bends on his patella
to slip on my shoe, as I sit upright above him on the examining table.
I'm Cinderella in silver sneakers. He becomes my prince in blue scrubs
who will help me to dance again.

But who's my Steady Eddy? The guy whose hands kept my Japanese
excuse for a car running until my daughter earned her college degree.
The mechanic, who picked me up one distress call after another
always bringing along his tank of gas.

EMPTY BOOTS

I'm feeling warm, downright hot. I hear sirens and fall in love with firemen.
I smell smoke. They've come to put out my heart's flame. Their ladders are high.
I'm afraid of heights. I want to know the feeling of being carried to safety.

But how could I ever let go?

EMPTY BOOTS

EMPTY BOOTS

A soldier in camouflage, a young man,
kneels in prayer like the men he has come to kill,
kisses the empty boots of a fallen comrade.
His soldier, a young woman.
Both toes of her dusty government issued shoes
are lined up so evenly, they look as if they're saluting.
She will not realize the college education
for which she enlisted, will never again
slip into a pair of slinky high heels
or kick them off as she peels away lingerie
on the way to the bedroom. Nor will she
chase after her kids in sneakers, or try
to balance motherhood with anything again.
Her rifle rammed upward in the sand,
helmet on the bayonet of her gun.

EMPTY BOOTS

THE WRITER & THE WARRIORS

Two Irishmen, McCourt and McNamara,
meet in a bar on their way to the great beyond—
Purgatory Pub, a watering hole for sinners.

McCourt, clearing his throat, chides with a brogue,
And what may I ask, brings your Harvard self here?

McNamara says softly, *Sent 58,000 American men
to their premature end. We didn't know our enemy. And you?*

McCourt, the smart ass admits, *Guess, I was after a little
too much of the excitement, never did listen to those collared
clerics with poles up their arses.*

The bartender, a warrior angel on temporary duty from above,
hums *Danny Boy*, missing his younger brothers, and asks

McCourt, didn't that book of yours sell 5 million copies?
'Tis true, who'd believe that swamp of a childhood would interest anyone?
*The angel on the seventh step that brought me then, can bring me back
home.*

The two knock down more than a few brown pints.
By now the bartender is singing *The pipes, the pipes are calling...*

Frank shouts, *Hey you, with the slicked back hair,*
then throws the first blow, *You, Mr. Secretary of Defense,
didn't you know better? You blaguard, body bagger!*

Bobbie, in his Harvard letter sweater, ever the reluctant warrior, mutters
No need to make trouble, thinking *I can take this skinny greenhorn.*

EMPTY BOOTS

James, the bartender bellows over the brouhaha,
I died over in 'Nam, before that sat around glued to the TV,
listening for my birthday to be linked to a lottery number.
McCourt get your sorry writer's ass out of here.
McNamara, not so fast...

The Writer: Frank McCourt,   1930- 2009
The Warrior: Robert McNamara,   1916- 2009
The Bartender: James Beck,   1947-1968

EMPTY BOOTS

WE'RE STILL HERE

We are here in 1963.
Women making fifty-nine cents for every dollar earned by men.
We are here, college girls after a B.S., not an MRS.
First female students living on campus at a Jesuit University.
Boys dorm over the cafeteria; our dormitory in another northern state.

We are here in 1977.
20th century suffragettes on capitol steps in Lincoln's Illinois.
Down to see passage of the ERA.* We are here with Phyllis Schlafly,
a lawyer with six kids, warning of unisex bathrooms. Husband complains
she isn't home enough. She cancels speeches. Time is all that passes.

We are here in 1984.
Headlines read, *Geraldine Makes the Scene.*
Nominated as the first female Vice President, doesn't hesitate a second.
A Catholic for Choice, proves she can cross muddied waters.
We think we've made it, shout out, until the ticket is beaten by a male movie star.

We are here in 2008,
Hillary makes her run. *Whitewater-gate, Monica-gate,* a president for a mate.
She's road- tested. Campaign posters block the view out the rear view.
She loses to an African American man raised by a single Mom.
The country is not yet ready for a woman.

We are here in 2015.
Sisters make seventy-seven cents for every dollar earned by men.
Our highlighted hair under military caps, surgical caps, pilot's hats.
Our retirement income $10,000 lower than Gramps. Is that progress?
We kick the voting machine; we just kick the machine.

* Equal Rights Amendment

FLIP-FLOPS

HOW TO HAVE A MEMORABLE SUMMER VACATION

Go with relatives
the one's you never get along with.
Pack outfits for each family member
for every weather eventuality. Mittens
might be called for. Sit on the carry-on
to close it, or tie with string if necessary.
Flip a coin to see who sleeps on the pull-out.
Wear shoes you have never worn before.
Ignore fevers, stomach pains,
bug bites and contagious diseases.
Who needs trip insurance?

Persuade others to climb the clock tower
visit unknown cathedrals—before noon.
After lunch, it's swim with jelly fish
followed by marathon shopping.
Peruse every museum starred in the guide book.
Afterwards, it's pop-quizzes on what's been learned.
Play Russian roulette with the gas tank.
Argue with local cops about non-posted speed limits.

Spend foreign currency in haste and freely.
Drive a stick shift minivan through mountain curves
though until now your life has been strictly automatic.
End with a splendid parade across a pedestrian bridge
in your mid-size automobile, no matter how
loudly passengers and natives scream.
No cameras are needed.
This trip will be memorable.

FLIP-FLOPS

WIMBLEDON, ENGLAND

Tennis, a prestigious and well mannered sport
I thought browsing the Wimbledon museum.
Gold cups and silver plates won on grassy courts.
I'm a grandstander wannabe in this British coliseum.

Walls hold gilded names of champions once in contention.
Now, I ask, should the list include McEnroe and Agassi?
Though Steffi and Martina deserve more than a mention
bad boys and real good girls expand the Lawn Club legacy.

Margaret and Billie Jean in my mind remain as queens.
Yet, does that matter in a game where love means nothing?
Federer won more matches with strokes that can't be seen.
Nadal gets to balls no one can, which must count for something.

Such a long trek on London's concrete streets for this solitary fan
to arrive at Center court, where green walls echo former gladiators.
Though as I stand on the same hallowed turf, more than
sneaker and racquet size separates winners from spectators.

FLIP-FLOPS

WE TURN SIXTY ON NANTUCKET

White caps curl, unfurl,
cerulean blue is the sky.
Purple hydrangeas ring
clapboard cottages, gray
as we have become. Again
we pilgrimage East to initiate
a decade as expected as the tides.
Unlike the one in our twenties
where we drove backwards on
the interstate, today we arrive
at the ferry with the precision
of a moon landing. Minnesota
Illinois, Ohio and Connecticut
the launching points. We embark
holding onto the luggage
of children, grandchildren.
Our friendships, as sturdy as fence
posts that guard this rocky shore.
We vacated the shells of youth.
The pearls at our centers
more lustrous, harder.
There are undercurrents.
Some hurricanes have touched land—
illnesses, betrayals, a son at war.
What's important is, we are with those
who knew us before, before life
left skid marks on our surfaces.
The end is nearer than the beginning.
Whatever old age does to these gems
of friendship, I never want to think
of them out of fashion, locked
in a musty jewelry box,
forgotten.

FLIP-FLOPS

VIEWING THE PIETA
Vatican City, Italy

Standing among strangers
surrounded by women
in mantillas, ball caps
summer straw hats
with black ribbon bands
crying, sniffling yet
I am bareheaded.
If men are here
I do not see them.

Mary is burdened
by folds of marble
head bowed, looking down
for all eternity at her son.
His body draped across her lap
her index finger points toward
the world to see Him.

I see only my friend
my neighbor holding
her collapsed son
in the cradle of her lap.
A tall hiker, a rock climber
only thirty years lived.
He completed suicide
in their garage, hanged
himself with expert knots.
She alone untied them.

Pray for all wild with grief.

SEPTEMBER'S PRAYER

THE MACK HOUSE
Nantucket, Massachusetts

I thought it was mine.
the way my four year old daughter
believed the book *The Lonely Doll* was hers.
Out of the library it came, each time
we biked over to get something to read
child in the carrier seat. Other books
selected, but this Dare Wright book
rode home until I bought it for her.
Finding it in the same place trip after trip
turned out better than owning it.

I thought it was mine.
Four summers vacations
idled away at this rental home.
Five bedrooms filled with friends
and friends of friends who became friends;
children and grandchildren running about
who became our children. Cisco beach
within walking distance, we're lulled to sleep
with crashing waves. An ocean of generosity
floated from room to room. The upper outside deck
so elevated, we felt we kissed the stars,
understood the complexities of the universe.

I thought it was mine.
I've rented movies, a car, even a bed
and a small .jazz combo. They never felt like mine.
I read *The Lonely Doll* to my granddaughters, hoping
I will grow out of this phase where we think
we possess all that we love.

SEPTEMBER'S PRAYER

MOTHER OF BRIDE EJECTED FROM CONVERTIBLE

Life did not flash, nor was there a crash.
God felt like a gentlemen caller
who opened the car door for me
so I became a passenger of the wind.
With my ear on asphalt, I heard traffic.
Friends screamed: *Stop! Stop! Stop!*
Green shrubbery, no sky
I thought I would be looking up when I die.
Head cradled, pulse taken, alive.
No glass, no seatbelts, a slight mishap.
College roommates comfort bride.
Alive, can walk down the aisle.
Nurses, they direct emergency room staff.
X-rays, now.

If my funeral was scheduled, I'm glad I was late.
Bridal shower later that afternoon.
My daughter's wedding day dawned glorious.
Black limo to the church.
Going to the chapel, sung at full lung.
Smile, sashay down the aisle.
My hands, knees & dress—all turquoise blue.

Dearest friends,
you, with whom I have shared bunk beds.
Come to my final farewell party, but not too soon.
Come in black tie & ball gowns
to sing off key, to toast our foolishness
our fifty year friendship, no accident.

SEPTEMBER'S PRAYER

SONNET DURING A STORM

I will love you until the twelfth of never.
 Water soaked snowflakes crack tree limbs in half.
I will love you until the hemispheres sever.
My love is stronger than Mother Nature's wrath.
Lights flicker inside, then outside; darkness claims.
Soon a thick white candle glows below
your pensive face in the sterling silver frame.
Over your chestnut hair, a bridal veil flows.
There's a storm between us, as you try to find your way.
Behind the window's glass, circuits fire, sparks careen.
Words and winds blow by; neither of us are easily swayed.
In this cold, blue bedroom, only your beauty can be seen.

Singular child, your face, the last visage I see tonight.
Be it the last one that I will behold on my final night.

SEPTEMBER'S PRAYER

DINNER WITH FRIENDS
Mary Ellen Mitchell, 12-31-1943 at rest 8-2-2015

We have reached midnight.
I glance over empty wine glasses
silver and china. Four dining chairs
askew, all at different angles
like doors swung open.

It's the green candles
under glass my eyes linger on.
I've never let them burn down so far.
12 inch tapers when this evening began.
Now less than an inch of candle left. They
drew down so quickly, I hardly noticed.

After dessert, Mary Ellen, our captivating
conversationalist, now with a cancer diagnosis
startles with a sorrowful soliloquy.
Three in her family left this earth in a span
of five years. As if sadness were a liqueur,
we sip it slowly. Table napkins turn into tissues.

At thirty, it was cartwheels in my living room.
Then vacations to islands, lately we're film festival junkies.
Fifty years of parties together, hangovers of laughter.
Now we wake to what might separate us. Alone
I sit in the dark staring at the flickering candles
as if they represent the last inch of life.

SEPTEMBER'S PRAYER

SEPTEMBER'S PRAYER
The days dwindle down to a precious few...

The leaves on trees are dwindling.
My height is descending.
Yet the sorrow is also diminishing.
These hands no longer reach out to touch you
have retired from the desire to want to.
But are cracked and empty as a snow shovel in June.

Blow in love that does not come to me in sorrow.
Cover the past the way fresh snow blankets
a rundown, familiar neighborhood
making its edges soft, crystalline, beautiful.

Chair-lift my body to a pinnacle.
Permit me to ski down life's last slopes
into the arms of family, cheering friends
known loves and loves yet to come
who will cushion my amateur landing
before life buries me.

Graduate course work at Trinity College in Hartford initiated Nancy Kerrigan's path to poetry. She is an alumnus of Wesleyan University's Writers Week, and workshops at the Frost Place in Franconia, New Hampshire. Her poetry appears in *Nantucket: A Collection*, Brett Van Ernst, editor. *Caduceus* Vol. 4, 5, 7 & 10 editor, Tony Fusco. *Rattle*, Vol.13, editor Tim Green, *The Breath of Parted Lips: Voices From the Frost Place*, editor, Sydney Lea. Her chapbook, *The Voices: The Poetry of Psychiatry* was published in 2009 by Finishing Line Press. She taught in the Schools of Nursing at Loyola University, St. Xavier University and Yale University. Poetry, for her is the artistic medium of choice to describe the complexities and ambivalences of the human mind.

www.ingramcontent.com/pod-product-compliance
Lightning Source LLC
LaVergne TN
LVHW041555070426
835507LV00011B/1091